Contents

Editor: Jeannette DeLisa
Photography: Mike Jones

Album Art © 1993 WARNER BROS. RECORDS INC.

HE SAID GO

Words and Music by
MARVIN L. WINANS

He Said Go - 4 - 2

4

Ad lib:
He said go and sin no more.
(He told her to go and sin no more.)
He said go and sin no more. (Jesus.)
He said go and sin no more.
(Oh, it's all right now, it's really all right.)
He said go and sin no more. (Oh yeah.)
He said go and sin no more. (I can believe it.)
He said go and sin, (No more.)
He said go and sin no more.
(Always remember what he said.)

THAT EXTRA MILE

Words and Music by
R. KELLY, MARVIN L. WINANS
and CARVIN WINANS

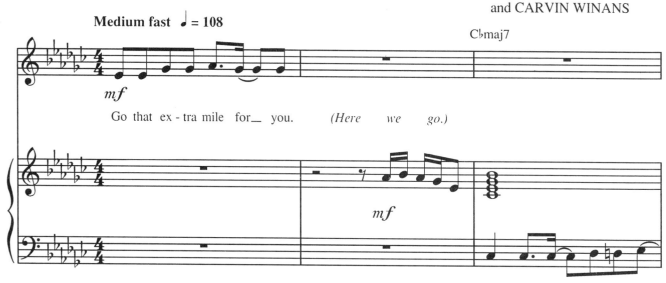

8

Verse 2:
Ooh, just when your mountain came tumbling down,
And your burdens were too hard to bear, oh hey,
That was his opportunity
To show you how much He cares.
And I know He'll do (He will do)
What He said (what He said).
All you got to do is believe in Him.
And I know (and I know)
His love is real (His love is real).
He has never failed me yet. *(To Chorus:)*

Ad lib. Chorus:
Go that extra mile for you,
I'm so glad to know.
Go that extra mile for you,
That He will, He will go that,
Go that extra mile for you,
And I'm gonna tell the world about it
His love, His love goes for it all.
On and on and on and on and on,

Never stops,
And it never quits.
It won't give up,
It'll never end.
For His love
For His love goes for it all.

IF HE DOESN'T COME TONIGHT

Words and Music by
MARVIN L. WINANS

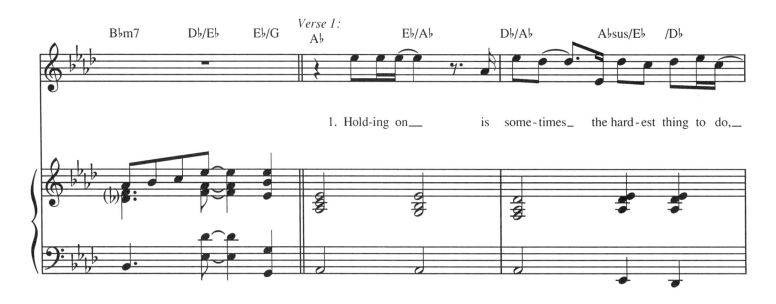

1. Hold-ing on___ is some-times___ the hard-est thing to do,___

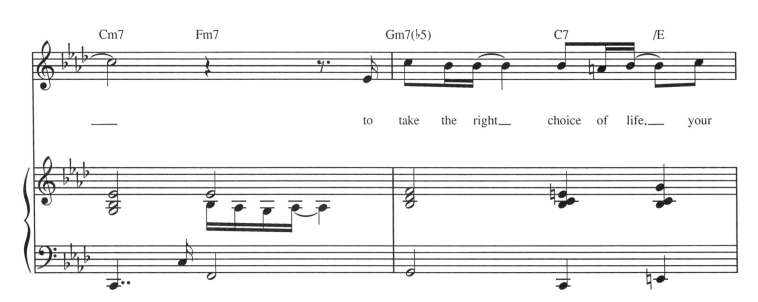

___ to take the right___ choice of life,___ your

If He Doesn't Come Tonight - 6 - 1

14

16

If He Doesn't Come Tonight - 6 - 5

ALL YOU EVER BEEN WAS GOOD

Words and Music by
MARVIN L. WINANS

Moderately fast, soulful rock ♩ = 116

Lyrics: 1. From the ear-li-est of my ex-ist-ence, un-til this pres-ent time, all

20

22

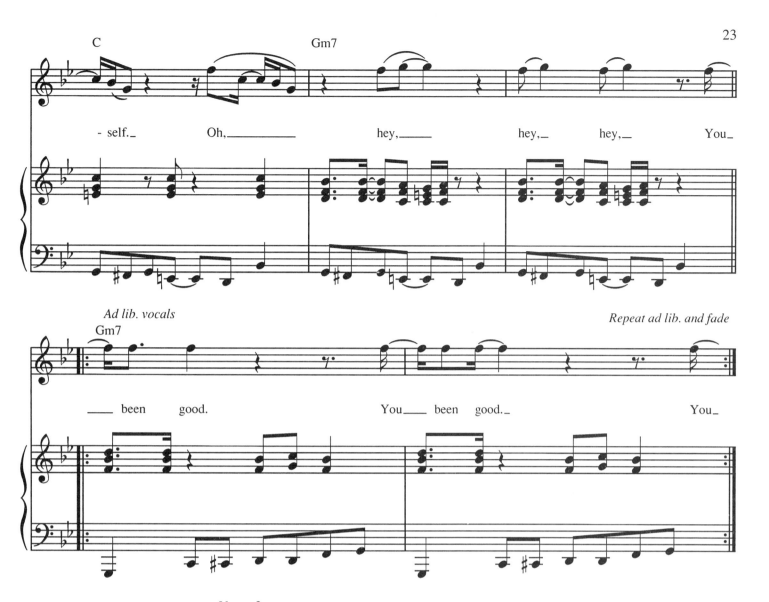

Verse 2:
I have had some hardships, plenty of sweat across my brow.
All You ever been was good, hey.
And if they ask me to testify a thousand years from now,
I'd say all You ever been was good, hey. *(To Chorus:)*

Chorus 2 (3 times):
You've been good; that's all You know how to be.
All you've ever been was good. Hey.

You been good; you've really been nice.
All you've ever been was good.

You've been good; you've really been nice.
All you've ever been was good.

Ad lib. vocals
You really really,
You really been good.
You been G-O-O-D.
You been mighty, mighty good to me.
You really been good.
You forgave me my sins.
You been my best friend.
When everyone left,
You didn't get upset.
You stayed by my side

To be my guide.
And I'm mighty glad to have,
Said I'm mighty glad to have,
'Cause You really been good,
You really been good,
You really been good,
I can't explain,
But I'm not ashamed.
And I'll tell the world,
Every man, woman, boy and girl
You really been good.

TRADEWINDS

Words and Music by
WILLIAM SALTER and RALPH McDONALD

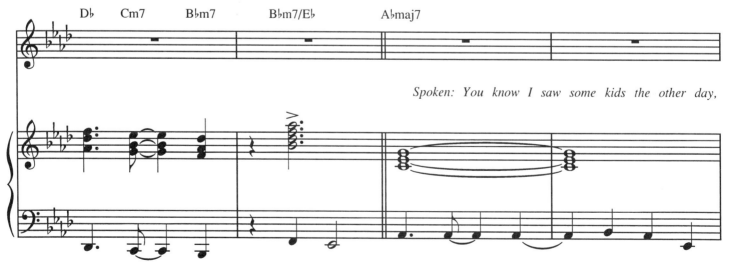

Tradewinds - 9 - 1

28

Tradewinds - 9 - 5

Verse 2:
Here I stand looking,
Looking around me,
While all around me
What do I see?
Young girls who soon become
(Girls who become)
Street walkers in the night,
(Walkers of the avenue)
Young boys with restless dreams
(Boys in the neighborhood)

Looking for a fight.
(Tell me what they're gonna do.)
Children both rich and poor,
(Children who are rich and poor)
They're searching for the truth.
If they don't find it,
God help tomorrow's youth.
They're caught in the tradewinds,
Tradewinds of time.
Ooh, they're caught in the tradewinds,
Tradewinds of time.

Marvin

Carvin

Ronald

Michael

IT'S NOT HEAVEN IF YOU'RE NOT THERE

Words and Music by
MARVIN L. WINANS

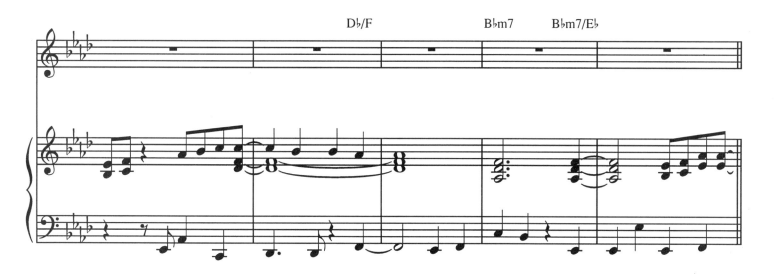

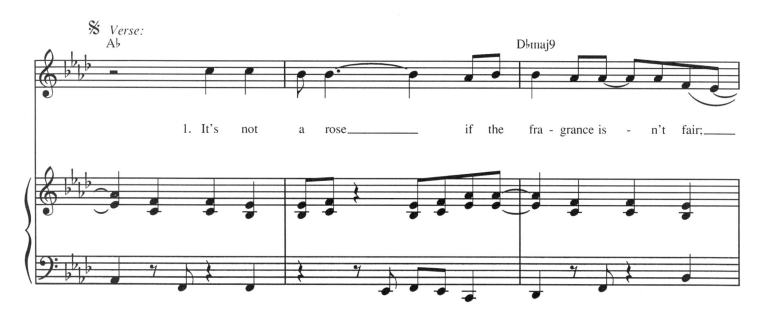

It's Not Heaven If You're Not There - 5 - 1

Verse 2:
It's not a leopard if it doesn't have spots;
It's not plethoric if it's not a lot.
Wouldn't be an eagle if it didn't soar through the air,
It's not heaven if You're not there.
Because You are heaven.

Bridge 2:
Some want to go to this glorious place,
Just to see the pearly gates.
Others wanna walk on the streets of gold,
To live forever and never grow old.

Verse 3:
It's not love if it doesn't share;
It couldn't be compassion if it does not care.
Wouldn't be an eagle if it didn't soar through the air,
It's not heaven if You're not there.
Let's say it again...

Verse 4:
It's not a rose if the fragrance isn't fair, no;
It's not a circle if the edges are square.
Here is something that I like to declare:
It's not heaven if You're not there.
(To Coda)

HEAVEN BELONGS TO YOU

Words and Music by
MICHAEL WINANS and REGINA WINANS

44

Verse 2:
Somebody told me that no eyes have never seen
All the beauty we'll behold.
Somebody told me all the streets are made of gold,
Where no one ever grows old.

Chorus 2:
Heaven, heaven belongs, heaven belongs to you.
(It's your for the asking.)
Heaven, heaven belongs, heaven belongs to you.
(Where the trees are the healing of the nation.)
Heaven, heaven belongs, heaven belongs to you.
(Where there's a river running through the middle.)
Heaven, heaven belongs, heaven belongs to you.
(In my father's house are many mansions.) *(To Bridge:)*

Ad lib. vocals
Heaven belongs to you. *(Background repeats)*
(Heaven belongs,)
(It's yours for the asking.)

(Heaven belongs,)
(I can hardly wait to go,)
(I got a new home there,)
(I got new friends there.)
(Heaven belongs.)
(It's mine, it's yours.)
(I got a new name there,)

(No shame there,)
Oh, oh, oh, oh, oh, oh, oh.

(Come on up, come on up a little.) *(Background repeats)* (higher.)
(You've got twelve gates to the city,)
(Twenty-four elders in the city.)
(No more pain, no more fears.)
(Angels singing, joy bells ringing.)
(It's yours, it's yours, it's yours.) *(Background repeats)*

(It belongs to you.)
(No one can take it away.)
(It's yours forevermore, it's yours forevermore,)
(He died so you could live in heaven,)
(Don't you wanna go.)
(It just belongs to you.)
(Heaven belongs, heaven belongs, heaven belongs.)

MONEY MOTIVE

Words and Music by
CARVIN WINANS

Moderate rock ♩ = 64

N.C.

Verse:

1. A few kids got to-geth-er for a walk on a

(bass solo, with rhythm)

sun-ny day;__

a strange man pulled up in a car and took

one a-way.__

He wrote a let-ter lat-er on to the mom for a

bank ac - count,_ a fan - cy car,_ and life seems sweet-er than hon - ey; but if you

D.S. 𝄋

got your gains_ by do - ing e - vil things,_ it's all get - ting read - y to pop.

Verse 2:
Johnny's dream was to stay in school, to be a doctor man,
Buy a house on a hill for his family to retire in.
He got entangled with the wordly good and was led astray;
To make a long story short, he dropped out of school and took the crooked way. *(To Chorus:)*

Verse 3:
When it came down to basketball, he was a natural;
He had one year left with the college team and he'd be turning pro,
But to make a little bread on the side, he went to betting games;
He got caught by the dean and the betting scheme went down the drain. *(To Chorus:)*

LOVE WILL NEVER DIE

Words and Music by
CARVIN WINANS

Love Will Never Die - 5 - 3

bye.   On-ly love can o - pen your eyes,_____   so look a -

round and let some - one know love's a - live.__   —   Look a -

round and let some - one know love's a - live.

Ad lib. vocal:
Only love, love, love.
Only love (only love can.)
Love can open your eyes.

PAYDAY

Words and Music by
CARVIN WINANS and WAYMAN TISDALE

Pay-day's com-ing. Well, it's pay-day, can I get a wit-ness? A new sha-bang,

—swing com-ing from the R, so check this. It's time to wake up and take heed to what I'm say-ing;

put your time in,—and there should-n't be no de-lay-ing. Don't throw the towel in once— you hear the bell ring; be

like the lit-tle train, I think I can, I think I can see. Hear ye, hear ye, step up and place your bid;

64

Verse 2:
Love's got your working overtime; (come on,)
So much pressure, yeah, you're losing your mind. (Yeah.)
You follow peace in all that you do,
And still you feel you are falling short of the rules.

Chorus 2:
Keep striving (come on),
Getting very close.
Don't stop now (yeah);
He's really on his way (come on).
Be a soldier (come on).
Keep holding up the cross.
Put your time in (yeah);
Payday's coming after while.

Chorus 3:
Keep moving (come on).
Getting real close.
Don't stop now (yeah);
He's really on his way (come on).
It's almost over (come on, come on).
Your soldiers of the cross.
Put your time in (come on, come on).
Payday's coming after while.
(To Coda:)